PRESENTED TO

Ruby Tunstall

FOR

P.E.

LOCHINVER
PRIMARY SCHOOL

27.6.12

First Encyclopedia of Our World

Felicity Brooks

Illustrated by David Hancock

Designed by Susannah Owen

Geography consultant: John Davidson

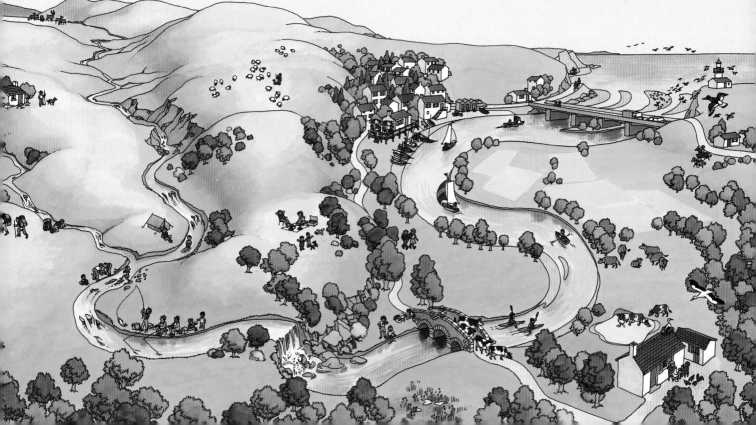

Usborne Quicklinks

The Usborne Quicklinks Website is packed with links to the best websites on the internet. For links and downloadable pictures for this book, go to:

www.usborne-quicklinks.com
and enter the keywords "our world"

You'll find links to websites where you can:
- See satellite images of Earth
- Learn about changing coastlines
- Follow a river from its source to the sea
- Explore a rainforest

Downloadable pictures
You can download lots of the pictures in this book and use them in your projects. All the pictures marked with a ★ are available to download at the Usborne Quicklinks Website. The pictures are for personal use only and must not be used for commercial purposes.

Internet safety guidelines
When using the internet please follow the internet safety guidelines displayed on the Usborne Quicklinks Website.

The recommended wesites in Usborne Quicklinks are regularly reviewed and updated, but Usborne Publishing Ltd is not responsible for the content or availability of any website other than its own. We recommend that children are supervised while using the internet.

Contents

Our planet

Our planet is called the Earth. It is the only planet where we know that plants, animals and people live. The large areas of land are called continents. Each continent is divided into smaller areas called countries.

This is a house...

in a town...

in a country...

in a continent on planet Earth.

Planet Earth travels around the Sun. It takes one year to go all the way around.

As it travels, the Earth spins around. It takes 24 hours to spin around once.

This is what you'd see if you went up in a spacecraft and looked at the Earth.

Swirling white clouds

Brown or green land

Blue seas and oceans

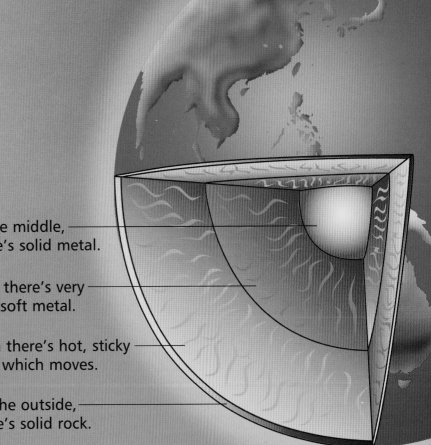

What's inside the Earth?

The Earth is made of rock and metal. If you could cut it open, you would see different layers inside. The picture on the right shows you what's inside the Earth.

In the middle, there's solid metal.

Next there's very hot, soft metal.

Then there's hot, sticky rock which moves.

On the outside, there's solid rock.

The atmosphere

The Earth is protected by an enormous blanket of gases, called the atmosphere. It stretches from the surface of the Earth over 600km (373 miles) into space. The sky you can see is part of the atmosphere.

The light, hazy blue on this photograph shows part of the Earth's atmosphere.

The atmosphere helps to keep the Earth warm at night.

In the daytime, it helps to protect you from the Sun's heat and light.

What's out in space?

It's hard to imagine how big space is. There are billions of stars, planets and moons in it. Some are so far away, it would take millions of years to reach them.

A star is a huge ball of hot gas.

A planet goes around a star.

A moon goes around a planet.

The Solar System

In our part of space, there are eight planets going around a star called the Sun. Together, they are known as the Solar System.

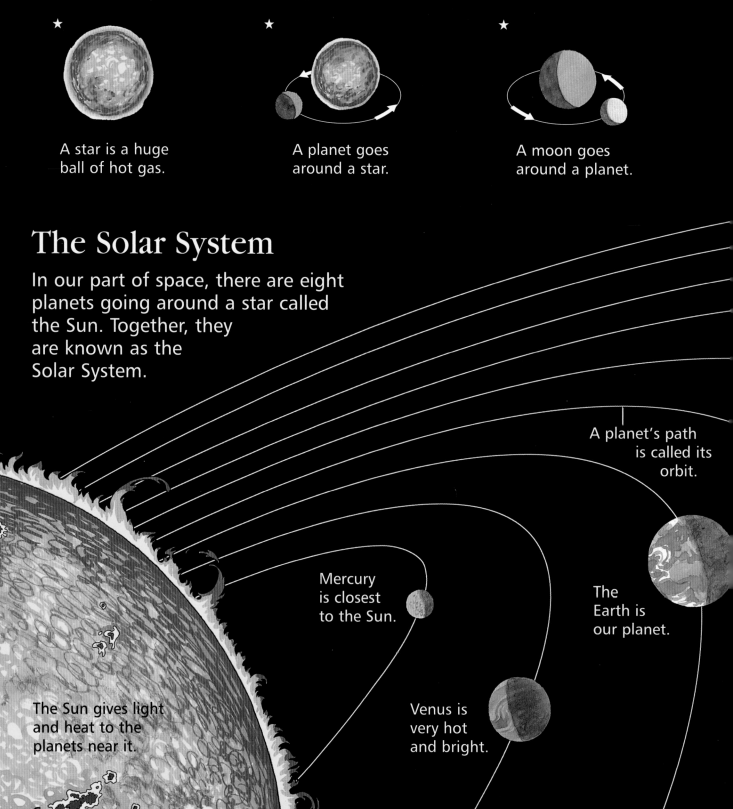

A planet's path is called its orbit.

Mercury is closest to the Sun.

The Earth is our planet.

The Sun gives light and heat to the planets near it.

Venus is very hot and bright.

Looking at space

If you look up at the sky at night, you can see the Moon, lots of stars and some of the planets. You could use binoculars or even a telescope to look at them all more closely.

Stars look tiny because they are so far away.

People use telescopes to see more clearly.

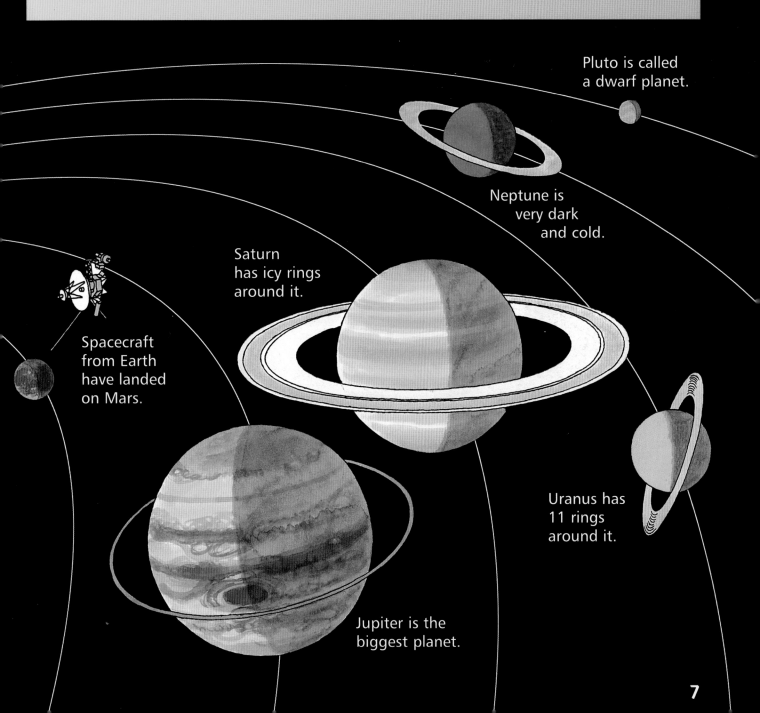

Pluto is called a dwarf planet.

Neptune is very dark and cold.

Saturn has icy rings around it.

Spacecraft from Earth have landed on Mars.

Uranus has 11 rings around it.

Jupiter is the biggest planet.

On the Moon

The Moon has no air and nobody lives there, but people have visited it six times. It took three days to get there in

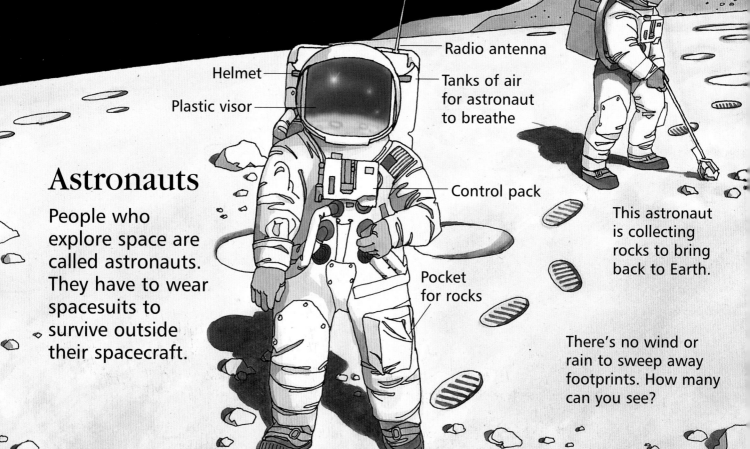

Helmet

Plastic visor

Radio antenna

Tanks of air for astronaut to breathe

Control pack

Pocket for rocks

This astronaut is collecting rocks to bring back to Earth.

There's no wind or rain to sweep away footprints. How many can you see?

Astronauts

People who explore space are called astronauts. They have to wear spacesuits to survive outside their spacecraft.

Going to the Moon

The astronauts went to the Moon in a rocket. They were inside the command capsule at the very top.

Five engines blast the rocket away from the Earth.

Command capsule

Stage 2 engines start up.

Stage 2 drops off.

Stage 1 drops off when its fuel runs out.

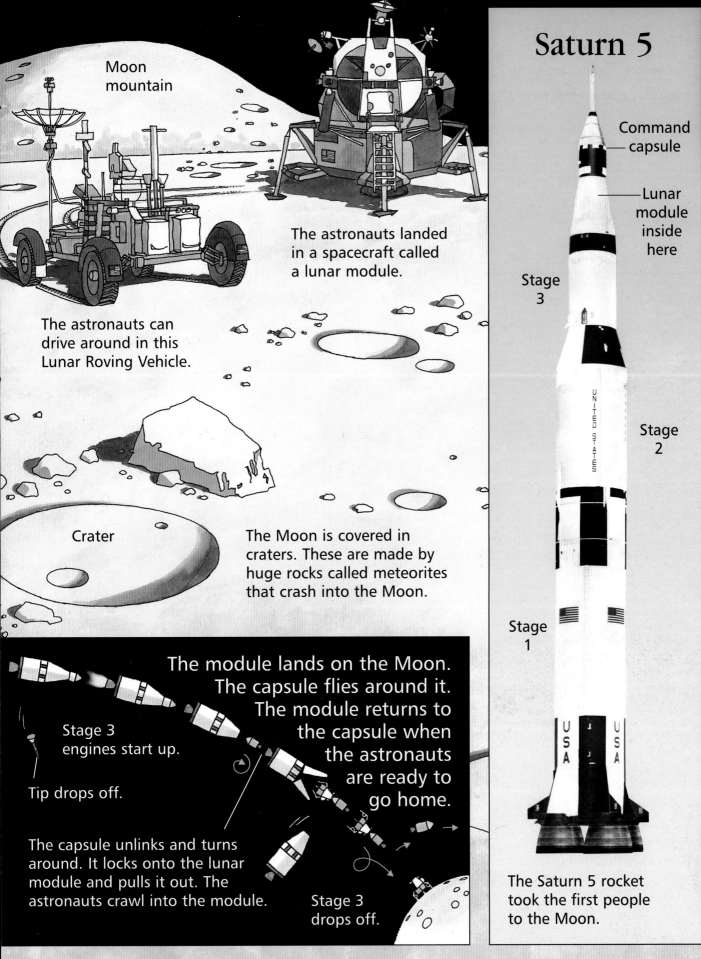

Moon mountain

The astronauts can drive around in this Lunar Roving Vehicle.

The astronauts landed in a spacecraft called a lunar module.

Crater

The Moon is covered in craters. These are made by huge rocks called meteorites that crash into the Moon.

The module lands on the Moon. The capsule flies around it. The module returns to the capsule when the astronauts are ready to go home.

Stage 3 engines start up.

Tip drops off.

The capsule unlinks and turns around. It locks onto the lunar module and pulls it out. The astronauts crawl into the module.

Stage 3 drops off.

Saturn 5

Command capsule

Lunar module inside here

Stage 3

Stage 2

Stage 1

UNITED STATES

USA USA

The Saturn 5 rocket took the first people to the Moon.

Landsat satellite

Looking at the Earth

Out in space there are spacecraft called satellites and space stations. They take pictures of the Earth which help us to learn about our planet.

Satellite pictures

Satellites fly around and around the Earth. There's no one in them, but they can send back information. Scientists turn this into pictures that help them see how hot the Earth is, or what the weather will be like. Satellite pictures can show anything from the beginning of a tropical storm to the size of a large city.

This satellite picture shows a hurricane (a big storm) about to hit the USA.

This shows the city of Washington DC, USA. The Potomac River is blue.

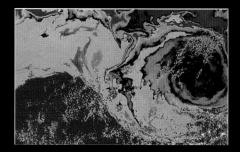

This shows the different temperatures of the sea. The hottest part is red.

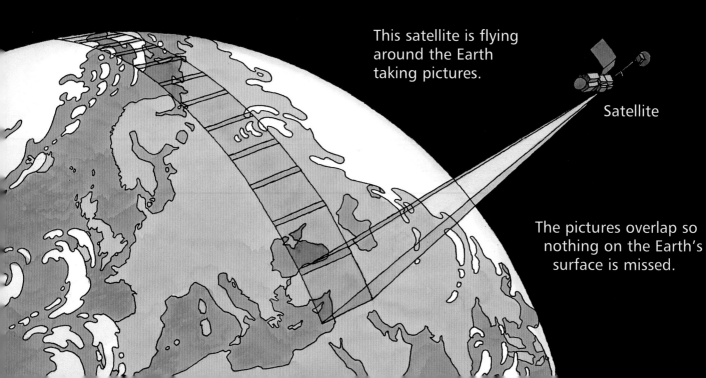

This satellite is flying around the Earth taking pictures.

Satellite

The pictures overlap so nothing on the Earth's surface is missed.

Space stations

Space stations go around the Earth about 400km (250 miles) up. People live and work on them. They take pictures of the Earth and other planets and stars.

Up to six astronauts live in this space station. How many can you see here?

★

These big wings are solar panels. They can make electricity from sunlight.

This is the control station.

In space, everything is weightless, so astronauts working on the space station float around.

The space shuttle

The space shuttle is like a plane that can travel into space. It blasts off like a rocket and glides back to Earth after a few weeks.

The shuttle takes people to space stations and puts satellites into space. Up to seven people can live in it.

Fuel tank

Rocket booster

When the shuttle lifts off it has a fuel tank and two rocket boosters. They drop off soon after.

Shuttle

USA   Challenger

Main engines

11

Day and night

When it is day for you, it is night for people on the other side of the world. When it is their day, it is your night.

This part of the Earth is in shadow. It's night here.

This part of the Earth is in sunlight. It's day here.

Sunrise

When your side of the Earth turns to face the Sun in the morning, the Sun is said to rise.

The Sun rising over a field

Sunset

When your side of the Earth turns away from the Sun in the evening, the Sun is setting.

The Sun setting over the sea

Turning Earth

Day changes to night, and night to day, because the Earth turns. As it turns, different parts face the Sun.

The part of the Earth with the USA on it is facing the Sun, so it's day in the USA.

A few hours later, the USA has turned away from the Sun, so it's night there now.

The Earth keeps turning all the time.

The Earth travels around the Sun this way.

After 24 hours, the Earth has turned all the way around, so now it's day again in the USA.

USA

Moon in the way

The only time it is dark in the day is when the Moon blocks out the Sun. This is called a total eclipse of the Sun. A total eclipse doesn't happen very often and it only lasts a few minutes.

This picture shows why an eclipse takes place.

The Sun, Moon and the Earth are all in a line.

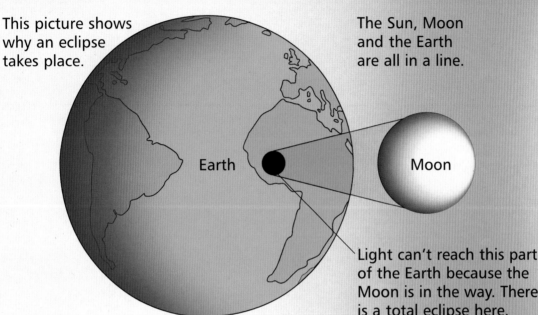

Earth

Moon

Sun

Light can't reach this part of the Earth because the Moon is in the way. There is a total eclipse here.

Make shadows

On a sunny day, you stop some sunlight from reaching the ground. This is what makes your shadow.

★

Try looking at your shadow on a sunny day. You will see that it always points away from the Sun. As the Sun rises higher in the sky in the morning, your shadow gets shorter. As the Sun sinks lower in the afternoon, your shadow gets longer.

Cloudy days

Even on a cloudy day the Sun is shining on your part of the Earth. You just can't see it because the clouds hide it.

Clouds like these may hide the Sun, but it is always there above them.

The seasons

Spring, summer, autumn and winter are the four seasons. The weather changes from season to season because of the way the Earth travels around the Sun.

The weather starts to get warm in spring.

The coldest season is winter. Nights are long. Days are short.

It's hot in summer. Nights are short and days are long.

After summer comes autumn. It starts to get cold again.

Earth words

Here are some words which are helpful when you want to know how the seasons work.

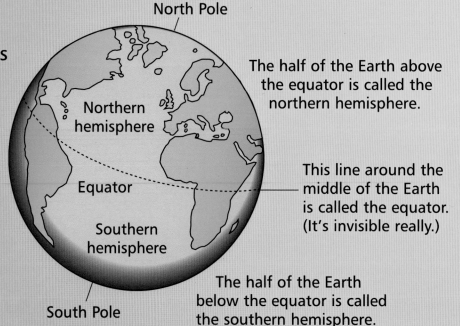

North Pole

The half of the Earth above the equator is called the northern hemisphere.

Northern hemisphere

This line around the middle of the Earth is called the equator. (It's invisible really.)

The poles are at the top and bottom of the Earth.

Equator

Southern hemisphere

The half of the Earth below the equator is called the southern hemisphere.

South Pole

Why the seasons change

The Earth is not upright as it goes around the Sun. It is tilted a little to one side. This means that during the year, first one half and then the other is nearer the Sun and gets more sunlight. This makes the seasons change.

Neither hemisphere is tilted towards the Sun in March. It's spring in the north and autumn in the south.

In December and January the southern hemisphere is tilted closer to the Sun, so it's summer there.

It's winter in the northern hemisphere in December, because that half is tilted away from the Sun.

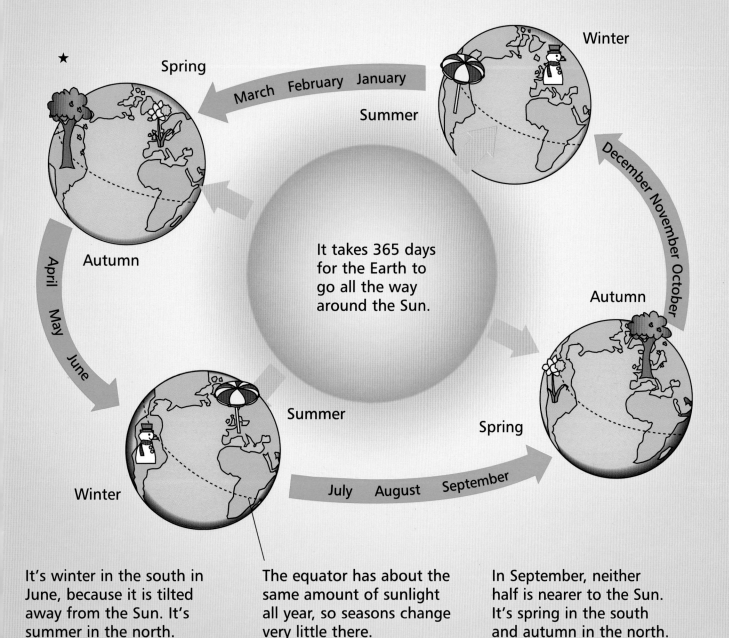

Spring

March February January

Summer

Winter

April May June

Autumn

It takes 365 days for the Earth to go all the way around the Sun.

December November October

Autumn

Winter

Summer

Spring

July August September

It's winter in the south in June, because it is tilted away from the Sun. It's summer in the north.

The equator has about the same amount of sunlight all year, so seasons change very little there.

In September, neither half is nearer to the Sun. It's spring in the south and autumn in the north.

The weather

There are lots of different kinds of weather. It can be sunny, windy, rainy or snowy. The three main things that make the weather happen are the Sun, the air and water.

The Sun gives heat to the Earth.

The air moves to make wind around us.

Water makes snow, rain and clouds.

The same rain

There isn't any new water on the Earth.
The same rain falls again and again.
Follow the numbers to see what happens.

3. The drops get bigger and join together into clouds.

2. Tiny, invisible drops of water rise up into the air.

4. When the drops get too heavy, they fall as raindrops.

1. The Sun heats up the water in rivers and seas.

5. Rivers run back into the sea.

What is snow?

Snowflakes fall instead of raindrops when it is very cold. They are made of tiny pieces of ice.

Every snowflake is different, but they all have six points.

Rainbows

You see a rainbow when the Sun shines through tiny drops of water in the air after it has rained. The sunlight divides into...

red
orange
yellow
green
blue
indigo
violet

Cloud clues

Clouds can give us clues about the weather.

Little, white, fluffy clouds mean good weather in summer.

Wispy clouds high in the sky show rain and wind may be coming.

Very tall, dark, fluffy clouds may bring thunderstorms.

Storms and winds

In a big storm, the wind blows very hard. There's usually lots of rain or snow. There may be thunder and lightning too. This picture shows what can happen near the sea when there's a very big storm.

The wind blows tiles off roofs.

Fallen trees block roads.

Chimneys sometimes break off.

Hats fly off.

Types of storms

A tornado is a spinning funnel of wind. It whirls along sucking up anything in its path.

Lightning is a big spark of electricity in the sky. Thunder is the noise that the spark makes.

A hurricane is a huge storm with lots of wind and rain. It can destroy towns and forests.

Trees bend and sway. Branches break off.

It's very hard to walk against the wind. You can't use an umbrella.

Waves smash into the land.

Flying objects may break windows.

Small rocks and pebbles are thrown onto the land.

Strong winds make enormous waves.

Boats are tossed around by the waves.

Rocks and fossils

There are lots of kinds of rocks. Some are made by heat inside the Earth. Others are made from sand, mud and pieces of dead plants and animals.

This is a fossil of a sea animal called an ammonite.

Rocky layers

Sand, mud and pieces of plants and animals that sink and settle at the bottom of the sea are known as sediment.

Layers of sediment

Layers of sediment build up slowly. Over millions of years, the bottom layers get squeezed and stick together to become sedimentary rocks.

Fiery rocks

Sometimes, hot, sticky rock from inside the Earth breaks through the surface.

Volcano

Hot, sticky rock

Hot, sticky rock pours out of a volcano. When it cools, it becomes hard. This kind of rock is known as igneous rock. Igneous means "fiery".

The Grand Canyon in Arizona, USA, is formed from layers of sedimentary rock.

This is a fossil
of a sea animal
called a trilobite.

Fossils

Fossils are the stony remains of animals that lived millions of years ago. Most fossils are found in sedimentary rock.

This is the fossil of a
sea creature called
a sand dollar.

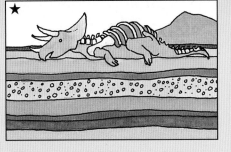

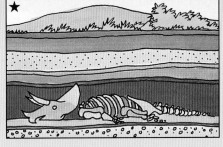

When an animal dies, its soft parts rot away, leaving its bones. If they sink into mud, they get covered in sediment.

Over millions of years, the sediment layers slowly harden into rock. This keeps the shape of the animal's bones in it.

Millions of years later, people sometimes find fossil bones or shells inside rocks. They have to dig them up carefully.

The Colorado River made the Grand Canyon. It started to wear the rock away millions of years ago.

Earthquakes

An earthquake happens when huge rocks deep under the ground slip and push against each other. This makes the ground above shake.

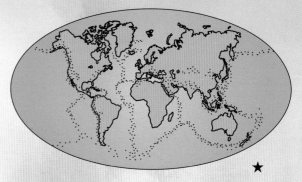

The red dots on this map show where earthquakes are most likely to happen.

Start of an earthquake

The place underground where an earthquake starts is called the focus. The effects of an earthquake are strongest on the surface right above the focus.

This house fell down in a big earthquake in California, USA, in 1994.

Earthquake effects

Most earthquakes are too weak to be felt by people, but some can cause great damage. The pictures below show some of the effects of an earthquake.

In a weak earthquake, hanging things, like birdcages, swing. Windows and dishes may start to rattle.

A stronger earthquake makes walls crack and pictures fall. Frightened people run outdoors.

In a very strong earthquake, buildings and trees fall down.

Staying safe

In countries where there are a lot of earthquakes, people are taught ways to stay safe. Children have earthquake-safety lessons at school.

Indoors, it is safest to shelter under a table. ★

Outdoors, you are safest in a big open space. ★

Earthquakes at sea

An earthquake that happens under the sea shakes the seabed. This sometimes creates huge waves, called tsunami (say "soonaamee").

In the deep ocean, tsunami are not dangerous and may pass under ships without anybody noticing. They only become enormous if they reach shallow water. Then they break and crash onto the land.

As the seabed moves, the sea above forms long, low waves. ★

If tsunami reach the coast, they are squeezed up into huge waves. ★

Earthquakes can cause huge waves, like this one. The biggest wave ever recorded was 525m (1720ft) high.

Volcanoes

A volcano erupts when hot, sticky rock from inside the Earth bursts through the surface. The hot rock, called lava, pours down the sides of the volcano and over the land.

This photograph shows a fountain of hot, sticky rock shooting out of a volcano.

Volcanic eruption

When a volcano erupts, lava comes out of a vent (opening) in the volcano's top or side. "Bombs" of rock may shoot up into the sky, and thick clouds of ash and gas may billow out. Sometimes a vent is in a hollow called a crater.

Lava is so hot it destroys everything it touches. The heat of the lava has set this wooden house on fire.

Volcano shapes

The lava cools and hardens into rock. Layers of lava and ash build up each time the volcano erupts, giving the volcano its shape. Some volcanoes are tall cones with steep sides and some are fairly flat with gentle slopes.

Many volcanoes are tall and steep. Their thick, sticky lava does not flow far before it hardens.

Some volcanoes are flatter. Their lava is runny. It spreads out quickly before it hardens.

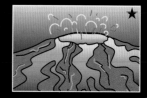

Sea volcanoes

There are lots of volcanoes under the sea. When one gets tall enough to appear above the waves, it makes an island.

This photograph shows clouds of steam and ash billowing from Surtsey, a volcanic island near Iceland.

A red-hot river of liquid rock is flowing down the side of this volcano.

Lava often moves quite slowly, so people usually have time to escape.

Alive, asleep or dead?

A volcano may be active (alive), dormant (asleep) or extinct (dead).

A volcano that erupts quite often is an active volcano.

A dormant volcano hasn't erupted for a long time, but may erupt again in the future.

An extinct volcano hasn't erupted for at least a million years. Some towns are built on extinct volcanoes.

Following a river

A river starts high up in hills or mountains. The water comes from rain or melted snow. It flows downhill until it reaches the sea. Follow this river to see how it changes.

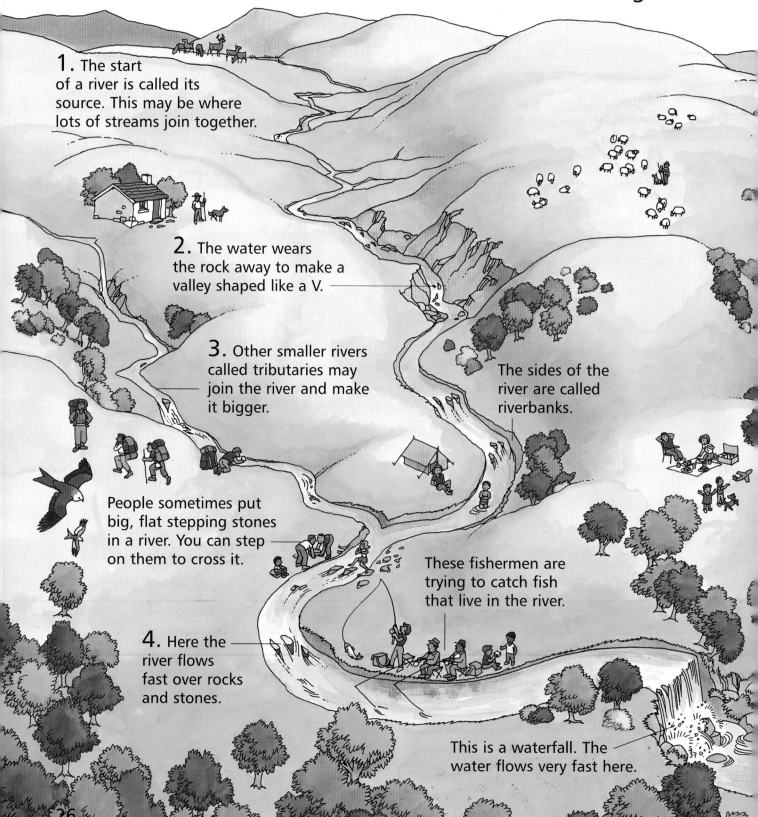

1. The start of a river is called its source. This may be where lots of streams join together.

2. The water wears the rock away to make a valley shaped like a V.

3. Other smaller rivers called tributaries may join the river and make it bigger.

The sides of the river are called riverbanks.

People sometimes put big, flat stepping stones in a river. You can step on them to cross it.

These fishermen are trying to catch fish that live in the river.

4. Here the river flows fast over rocks and stones.

This is a waterfall. The water flows very fast here.

Waterfalls

A waterfall forms where a river flows from hard rock to soft rock. The water wears away the soft rock faster than the hard rock. This makes a big step.

This photograph shows water rushing over the Kanchan Waterfall in Cambodia.

9. The place where a river joins the sea is called the mouth of the river.

Lots of birds feed on the little animals that live in the sand.

Bank of sand

7. The river carries lots of sand and mud to the sea.

8. The river drops most of its sand and mud when it reaches the sea.

6. The river is deeper and wider on the outer edge of the bend.

5. Here the river starts to flow in big loops called meanders.

Floods

A flood is water that covers land that is usually dry. Floods may happen when there is a lot of rain in a short time, or when it pours with rain for a long time. Rivers get too full and spill onto the land.

As the water rises, people try to stay safe on roofs.

More floods

A flash flood is a sudden rush of water. It happens when a lot of rain falls in one place in a short time.

Huge waves can also cause floods. They are made by storms or by undersea volcanoes or earthquakes.

Some floods happen when snow and ice melt. The soil is still frozen so water cannot soak into it.

Not all the rain can seep into the ground, so it covers the land.

These people are trying to stop the water. They are making a wall of bags filled with sand.

Monsoon floods

The monsoon is a wind. In Asia, it blows one way all summer and the other way all winter. In summer it brings very heavy rain from the oceans.

The monsoon rain often floods cities and homes but people try to carry on with their lives as normal.

Farmers need the monsoon rain for their crops to grow. Plants such as rice grow well in the wet soil.

These people were stranded when their house became surrounded by the flood water. They are escaping in a boat.

Mountains

Mountains form over millions of years. Vast pieces of rock on the Earth's surface push against each other and force part of the land up into mountains.

A group of mountains is known as a range. These mountains are part of a range called the Rocky Mountains in Canada.

Parts of a mountain

Some mountains have snow on their peaks (tops) all year. The level where the snow ends is called the snowline.

Trees often grow on a mountain's lower slopes, but it's too cold for them to grow above a certain level. This is known as the treeline.

A gap between two peaks in a range is called a pass.

Peak

Treeline   Snowline

Pass

This picture shows the parts of a mountain.

Avalanche!

An avalanche begins when a huge slab of snow starts to slide down a mountain. A heavy snowfall or a sudden change in the weather can cause an avalanche. The snow rushes downhill and buries everything in its path.

This small village has been hit by an avalanche. Some houses are completely covered in snow.

Mountain life

Some plants and animals can live on mountains. They need to be able to survive in very cold temperatures and strong winds.

★ Mountain flowers such as purple saxifrage grow in short, round clumps.

Conifer trees have tough, narrow needles instead of broad leaves. ★

Golden eagles build their large nests on mountain rocks and ledges.

★

★ Mountain hares have thick fur that turns white in winter.

The seashore

The seashore is where the sea meets the land. On most shores the sea moves up and down the beach. This is called the tide. At low tide a beach is dry. At high tide it's covered by water.

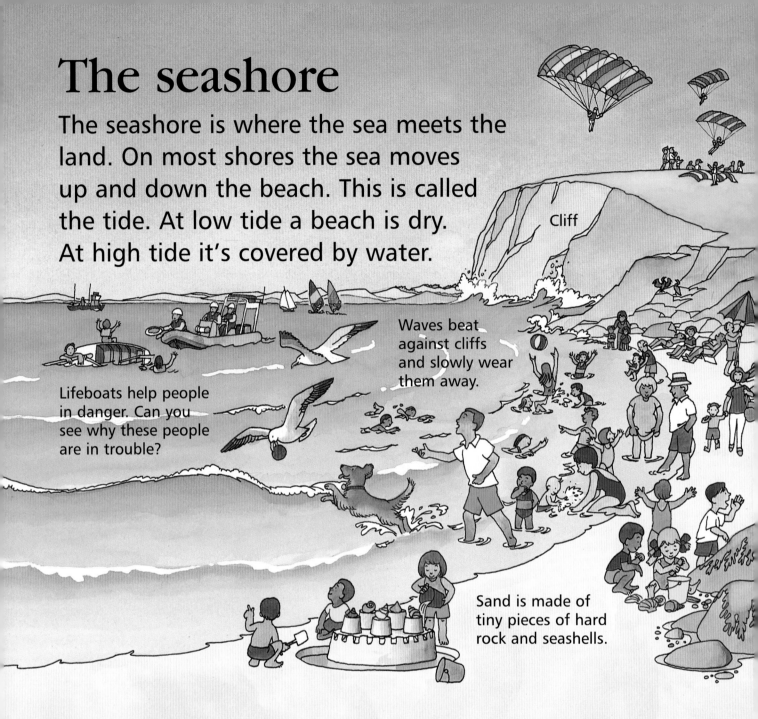

Cliff

Waves beat against cliffs and slowly wear them away.

Lifeboats help people in danger. Can you see why these people are in trouble?

Sand is made of tiny pieces of hard rock and seashells.

Headlands, cracks, caves and blowholes...

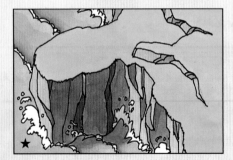

★ This headland is made of hard rock. The sea can't wear it away as fast as the rock around it.

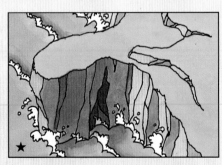

★ Waves crashing onto the headland made this big crack. Little by little they will widen it into a cave.

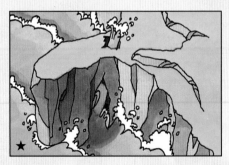

★ Waves have worn through the top of this cave and made a blowhole. Water spurts out at high tide.

At night, a lighthouse shows ships where there are dangerous rocks or cliffs.

Boulders are big rocks which have fallen off the cliff.

Pebbles are bits of rock which the sea has worn smooth.

Pools of water are left among the rocks when the tide goes out. Lots of sea creatures live in them.

Seaweed

. . .arches, stacks and stumps

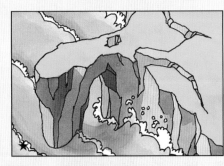

When waves wear away caves on both sides of a headland, the caves may meet and make an arch.

The waves keep pounding the arch until its top falls off. A pillar of rock called a stack is all that's left.

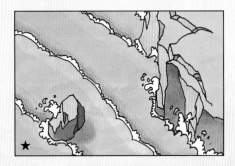

After many years all that is left of the stack is this stump. The rest has been worn away by the waves.

33

Seas and oceans

Seas and oceans cover almost three-quarters of the Earth. There are five oceans and lots of smaller areas of salty water, called seas, bays and gulfs.

The Pacific covers almost a third of the Earth. This is what it looks like from space.

This map of the world shows the oceans.

All of the oceans are joined up.

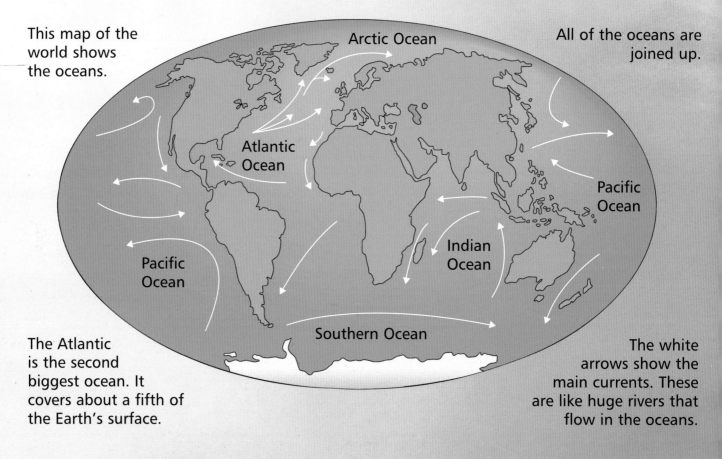

Arctic Ocean

Atlantic Ocean

Pacific Ocean

Pacific Ocean

Indian Ocean

Southern Ocean

The Atlantic is the second biggest ocean. It covers about a fifth of the Earth's surface.

The white arrows show the main currents. These are like huge rivers that flow in the oceans.

Catching fish

There are many ways of catching sea fish. This boy is using a fishing rod.

This boat drags this net along to catch fish which live near the seabed.

These are called creels. They are used to catch crabs under the sea.

Exploring the ocean

There's plenty to look at under the sea. People explore it in small submarines or by going diving.

Can you see some pirate treasure and an old anchor?

Most animals and plants live near the surface where it's light and warm.

It is icy cold and dark in the deepest parts of the ocean. A few animals live there.

Tuna

Dolphins

These divers carry tanks full of air for them to breathe.

Shipwreck

Shark

Seal

Humpback whale

Herrings

Green turtle

Octopus

Sperm whale

Giant squid

Angler fish

This is a submersible. It can dive deep into the sea with three people inside it.

Gulper eel

Tripod fish

Under the sea

The bottom of the sea is called the seabed. Under the water there are plains, mountains, volcanoes and valleys.

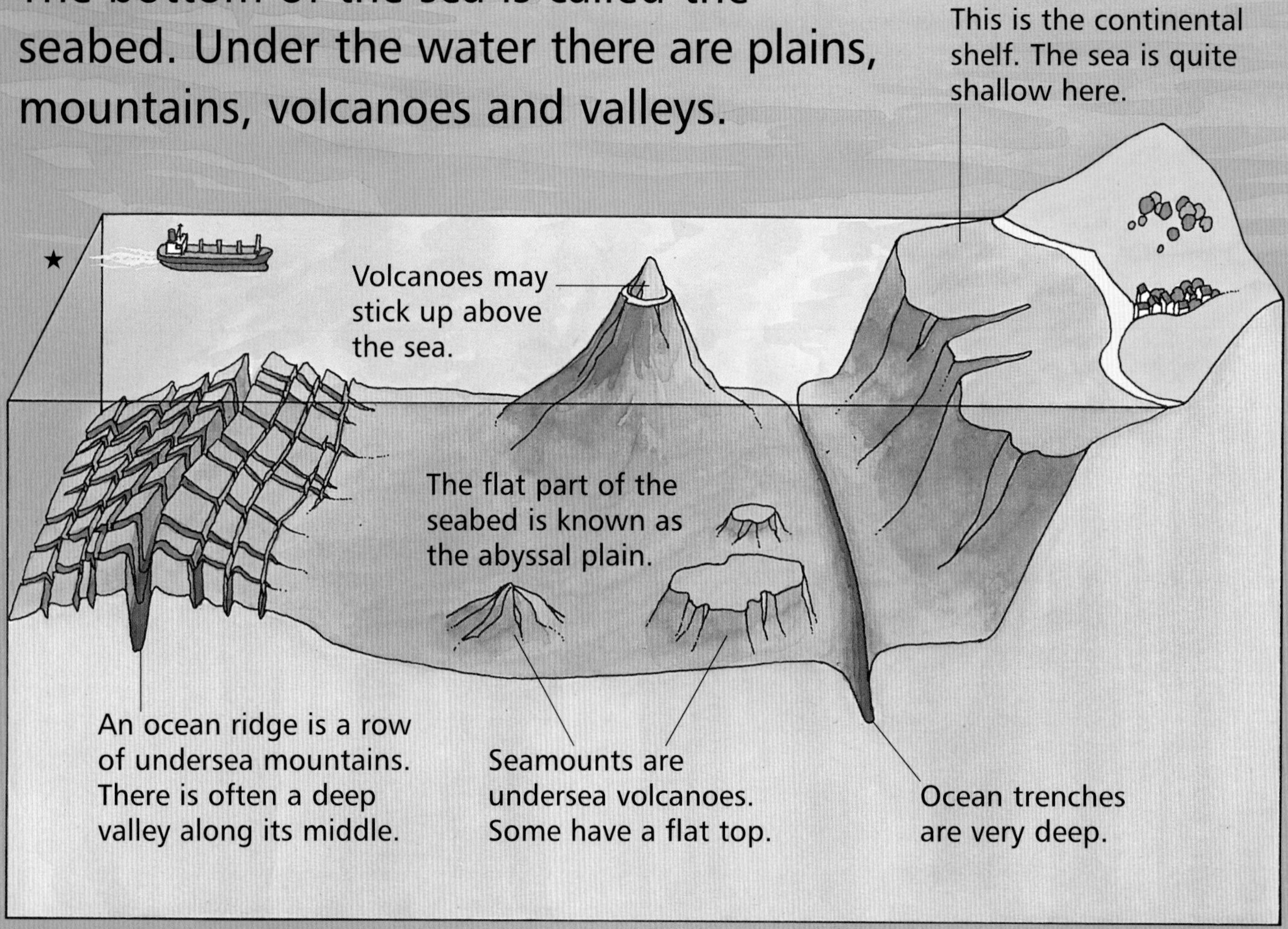

This is the continental shelf. The sea is quite shallow here.

Volcanoes may stick up above the sea.

The flat part of the seabed is known as the abyssal plain.

An ocean ridge is a row of undersea mountains. There is often a deep valley along its middle.

Seamounts are undersea volcanoes. Some have a flat top.

Ocean trenches are very deep.

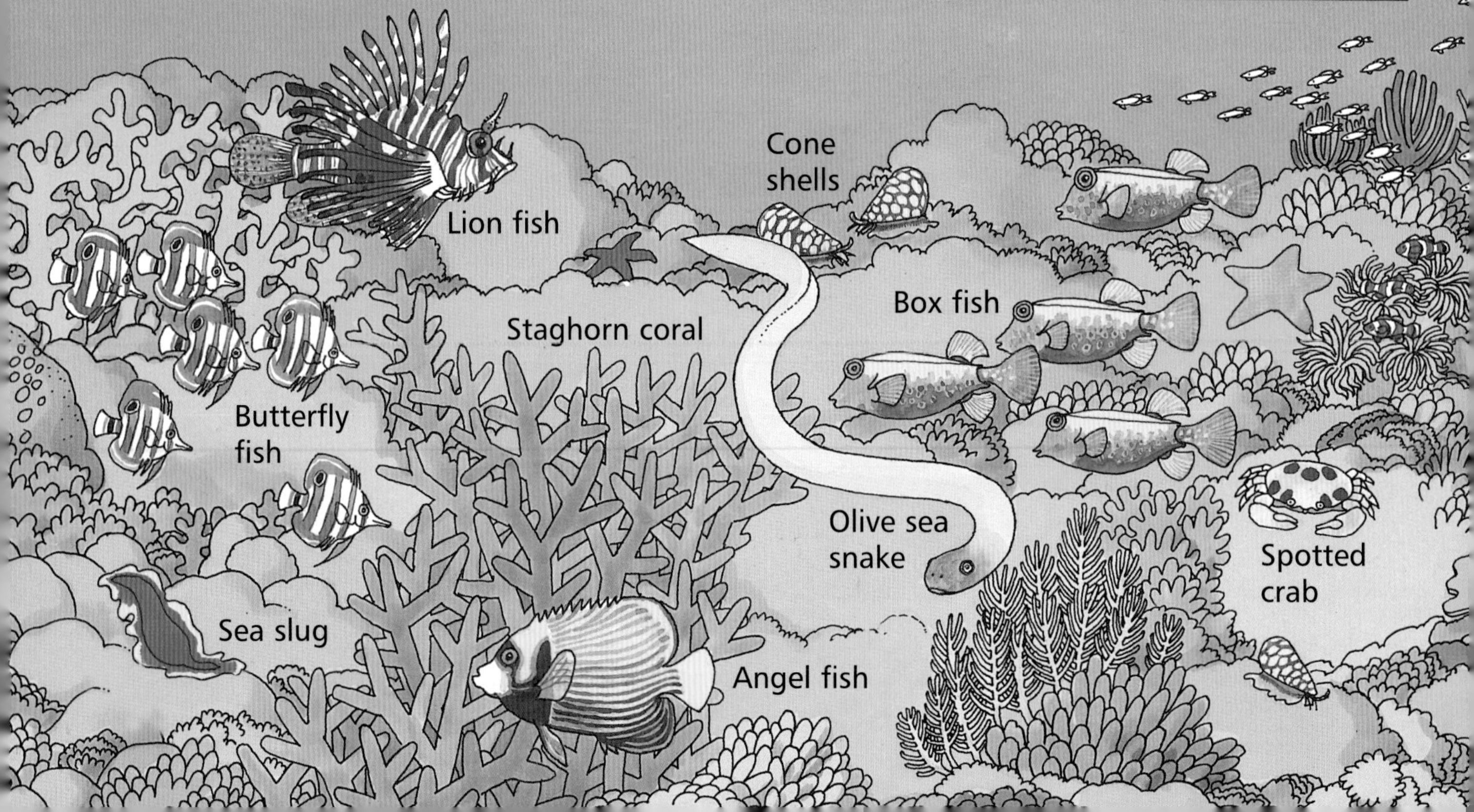

Lion fish

Cone shells

Box fish

Staghorn coral

Butterfly fish

Olive sea snake

Spotted crab

Sea slug

Angel fish

Coral reefs

Coral reefs grow in warm, clear, shallow water. They are home to thousands of plants and animals.

Can you spot two divers?

Clown triggerfish

Barracudas

Harlequin tusk fish

Anthiases

Sea fan

Sea wasp

Coral trout

Coral cod

Moray eel

Surgeon fish

Giant clam

Moorish idols

Sea anemones

Starfish

Brain coral

Under the ground

There's a world beneath your feet that you don't see. If you could look under the ground, here are some things you might spot.

Moles tunnel in the soil. They make molehills when they come up to the surface.

Soil near the surface is called topsoil.

Rabbits live in burrows.

Roots stop trees from falling over. They suck up water from the soil, along with other things the tree needs to grow.

Little creatures

Many small creatures live in the topsoil. Here are some you might see.

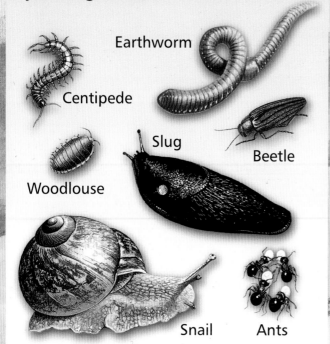

Centipede

Earthworm

Slug

Beetle

Woodlouse

Snail   Ants

Ancient pot

There may be things buried in the soil that belonged to people long ago.

Under the thick layer of soil, there is solid rock.

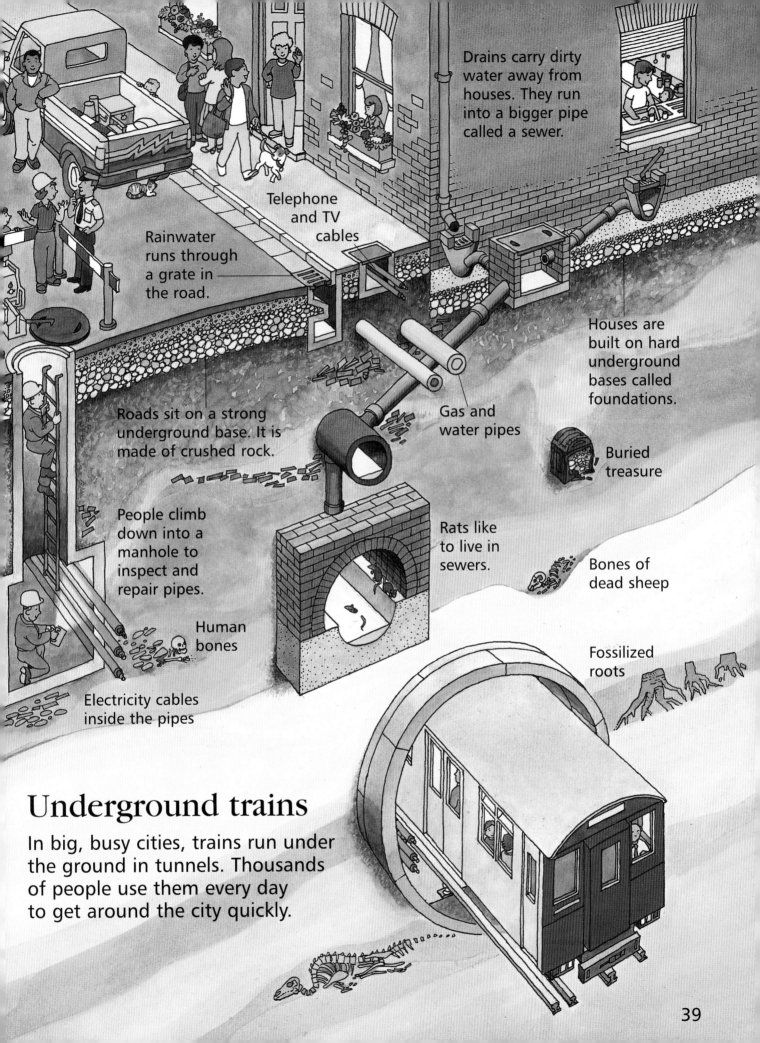

Drains carry dirty water away from houses. They run into a bigger pipe called a sewer.

Telephone and TV cables

Rainwater runs through a grate in the road.

Houses are built on hard underground bases called foundations.

Roads sit on a strong underground base. It is made of crushed rock.

Gas and water pipes

Buried treasure

People climb down into a manhole to inspect and repair pipes.

Rats like to live in sewers.

Bones of dead sheep

Human bones

Fossilized roots

Electricity cables inside the pipes

Underground trains

In big, busy cities, trains run under the ground in tunnels. Thousands of people use them every day to get around the city quickly.

Caves and caverns

A cave or cavern is like an underground room with walls made of rock. Some caves are just below the surface. Others are very deep underground.

Caves like this one form slowly over many thousands of years.

How caves are made

Each time it rains, the rainwater seeps through cracks in the rock.

Over a long, long time, the water dissolves the rock and wears it away.

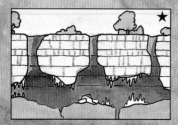

When the level of the water drops, empty caves and passages are left.

This man is one of a group of French cavers who climbed down into this cave in Hunan, China, to explore it.

40

Rocky shapes

Some caves are full of strange, rocky shapes. These are made by water which has trickled through the rock and dissolved some of it. When the water drips, it leaves behind some of the dissolved rock. This builds up very slowly to make the rocky shapes.

★ Stalactites hang from the roof.

Stalagmites form on the floor.

Sometimes stalactites join up with stalagmites.

Cavers

Cavers are people who explore caves for fun, or to find out more about them. Cavers often squeeze through narrow passages or wade through deep water to reach a cave. They have special clothes and equipment to keep them safe and help them explore the caves.

Helmet with lamp

Thick overalls

Strong rope

Waterproof boots

Bears, bats and bison

Brown bear

★

Brown bears and black bears sleep inside caves through the winter.

Horseshoe bat

★

Many kinds of bats spend the winter in caves. They fly out in the spring.

★

Cave painting of a bison

A long time ago, people lived in caves. They made pictures on the walls. These pictures help to tell us what life was like then.

In the desert

Deserts are the driest places in the world. Sometimes it doesn't rain for many years. Most deserts are very hot in the day, but cool at night.

Sahara Desert

AFRICA

Deserts cover over a quarter of the Earth's land. The biggest is the Sahara Desert in North Africa.

Desert homes have flat roofs, and small windows to keep out the sun.

Palm trees

An oasis is a place where there is water so plants can grow.

Camels can last a week without water.

Euphorbia plant

Antelopes

Most deserts are rocky and bare. Only parts of them are covered in sand.

Sandgrouse

Jerboas hop along like miniature kangaroos.

Desert plants

Many desert plants have long roots, and stems which can soak up water. Some, like the barrel cactus, can store water inside.

Before rain

After rain

A barrel cactus swells with water when it rains.

A giant saguaro cactus may live for hundreds of years.

When the wind blows, the sand piles up into hills called sand dunes.

Lanner falcon

Desert people live in groups and move from place to place. They keep sheep, goats and camels.

Fennec foxes have huge ears which help them to lose body heat.

Saw-scaled adders slither along with an S-shaped wiggle.

Grasslands

Plains, or grasslands, are big areas of land covered in grass. Bushes and some trees may grow there too. The picture below shows part of a grassland in Africa.

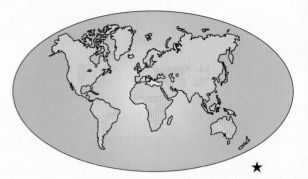

Grasslands, shown in orange on the map, cover about a quarter of the Earth's land.

Baobab trees can store water in their trunks.

Ostriches

Rhinos

Elephants

Thousands of insects called termites make these big mounds.

Baboons live in large groups called troops.

Lions live in groups called prides.

Weaver birds make complicated nests.

Acacia tree

Wildebeest

Hyenas

Tourists come in trucks and buses to see the animals.

44

Vultures

Tourists in a
hot air balloon

The dry grass catches
fire easily. It grows
again when it rains.

Giraffes

Lots of animals come
to a waterhole to
drink and stay cool.

Antelopes

Warthogs

Zebras

Cheetahs

Prairies and steppes

There are many names for
grasslands around the world.
Grasslands in Russia are known
as steppes.

In North America, grasslands are
called prairies. Most prairies are
now used as farmland. Wheat
grows well there.

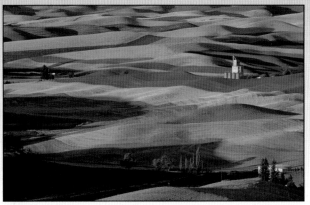

Huge fields of wheat stretch across the
grasslands of North America.

In the rainforest

Thick, green rainforests grow in hot, wet places near the equator. It is warm all year there and it rains nearly every day. Rainforests are home to thousands of different plants and animals.

SOUTH AMERICA

Amazon River

The biggest rainforest is the Amazon Rainforest in South America. The Amazon River runs through it.

Rainforest trees grow very tall.

Spider monkeys

Morpho butterfly

Lichen

Arrow-poison frog

Jaguar

Hummingbird

Orchids

Plants on trees

Many rainforest plants grow on the branches of trees where there is more light than on the ground.

Ferns

Scarlet macaws

Toucans

Howler monkeys

Lianas are plants with long stems like ropes.

Bromeliad

Sloths move very slowly.

Capybaras look like large guinea pigs.

Caiman

These big buttress roots hold the tall trees upright.

Giant armadillo

Scarlet ibis

Anacondas are huge snakes.

Matamata turtle

Giant water lily leaves

Icy world

The places near the top and bottom of the Earth are called polar regions. They are very cold. Huge areas of land and sea are covered in ice and snow.

The area around the North Pole is called the Arctic.

The area around the South Pole is called the Antarctic.

Polar ice

The ice in the polar regions forms flat sheets and glaciers, and covers high mountains. In the summer, some of the ice melts, but in the winter it freezes solid again.

What is an iceberg?

Icebergs are huge chunks of ice floating in the water. The small top part, or tip, floats above the water. The rest is hidden below. The pictures on the right show how an iceberg forms.

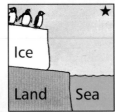

Ice

Land   Sea

A sheet of ice moves over the land to the sea.

At the sea, the ice moves out over the water.

A piece of ice breaks off. This is an iceberg.

48

Life near the poles

Not many people live in the Arctic, compared with most other areas of the world. No one lives in the Antarctic all the time, but scientists go there to study its animals, weather and land. Tourists go to both places to climb, ski, and see the wildlife.

Many penguins live in the Antarctic. They have a thick layer of feathers and fat to keep out the cold.

Surviving the cold

Animals that live in the polar regions have to survive in very cold weather. They must keep warm and find food in icy conditions.

Polar bears make long journeys over the Arctic snow and ice in search of seals, birds, fish and plants to eat.

★

Antarctic icefish have special liquid in their blood to stop it from freezing.

★

Walruses live in the Arctic. A layer of fatty blubber under their skins keeps them warm.

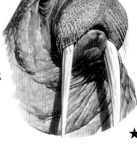

★

Weddell seals hunt for food under the Antarctic ice. They make breathing holes in the ice.

★

Rivers of ice

Solid rivers of ice that move very slowly downhill are called glaciers. They are found in places where it is always very cold and shady. Glaciers are made from snow that falls at the top of a mountain and turns into ice.

Deep snow builds up in hollows high up in the mountains.

The top layers of snow press down on the bottom layers and turn them into solid ice.

The ice moves slowly down the mountain as more ice builds up behind it.

The glacier carries stones and pieces of rock down the mountain.

Other smaller glaciers may join the main one.

Deep cracks in the ice are called crevasses.

The glacier melts as it gets warmer farther down the mountain.

When glaciers melt

A long time ago there were far more glaciers than today. When they melted they left valleys that look like this.

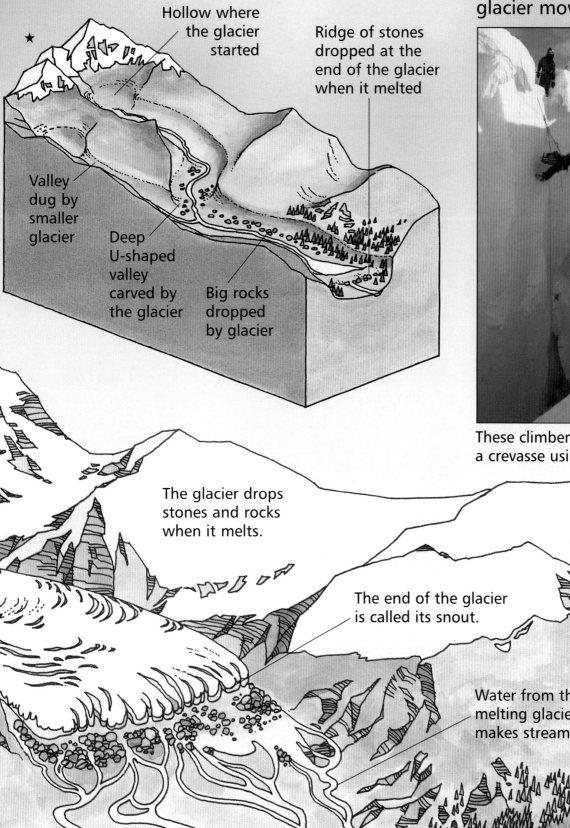

★

Hollow where the glacier started

Ridge of stones dropped at the end of the glacier when it melted

Valley dug by smaller glacier

Deep U-shaped valley carved by the glacier

Big rocks dropped by glacier

The glacier drops stones and rocks when it melts.

The end of the glacier is called its snout.

Water from the melting glacier makes streams.

Crevasses

Crevasses in glaciers can be 60m (200ft) deep. They often close or open up when the glacier moves.

These climbers are exploring a crevasse using ropes.

Cities and towns

A city is a big, busy town where many people live and work. About half of all the people in the world live in a town or city. Many cities have tall buildings because of the shortage of land.

Living together

People living in towns and cities need houses, schools, hospitals and shops. They also need places where they can enjoy themselves, such as parks and cinemas. There must be work for people to do, too, so they can afford to live there.

As in many cities, these buildings in New York, USA have many floors on top of each other to use less land.

★ In the middle of a city, there are often large and well-known shops as well as many smaller ones.

★ Cities have restaurants, museums and cinemas where people can enjoy themselves.

City problems

Many people like living in a city. There is plenty to do, and shops and schools are nearby. But city life is not always easy. For example, it can sometimes be hard to find a job, or a home that you can afford to live in.

There are often too many cars in cities. They jam the roads and fill the air with fumes.

Sinking city

Around 21 million people live in Mexico City. All these people use vast quantities of water for drinking and washing. It is pumped from the underground lakes found beneath Mexico City. So much water has been pumped that now the city's streets are sinking a little deeper each year.

Most cities have parks for people to enjoy. This is New York's Central Park.

Useful Earth

We depend on the Earth to survive. It gives us food, water, air and all we need for building and making things. It also gives us the fuel we need for cooking, heating and making machines and engines go.

Sand is used to make glass.

We eat many kinds of plants. Some are made into material, such as cotton, for clothes. Others are made into medicines.

Coal and oil

Coal is made from rotted trees and plants from millions of years ago. Oil began as tiny, dead sea animals. Coal and oil are taken from under the ground and used as fuels, but they are also used to make lots of other things.

Oil and natural gas come from under the ground or under the seabed. People drill for them from rigs.

Coal can be used to make paint, plastic, perfume, soap and the "lead" in pencils.

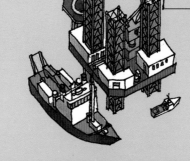

Oil rig

Oil can be used to make dishwashing liquid, plastic, petrol and dye.

Wood from trees can be made into many things, such as furniture and paper.

Animals give us leather and wool as well as milk, meat and eggs.

Metal, coal, stone, clay and other useful things are dug out of the ground in places called quarries or mines.

Fishing boats catch fish from the sea.

Non-stop power

Oil, gas and coal may one day run out. There are many other ways of making power. They use things that will not run out, such as wind, water and sunshine.

These are wind turbines. The turning blades drive machines to make electricity.

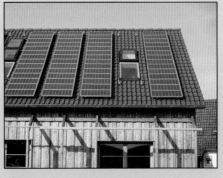

Solar panels can soak up heat from the Sun and use it to make water hot.

Like the wind, flowing water can also drive turbines to make electricity.

The web of life

Plants, animals and people depend on other living things to survive. Animals and people eat plants, and some animals and people eat other animals. A food chain shows how plants and animals are connected.

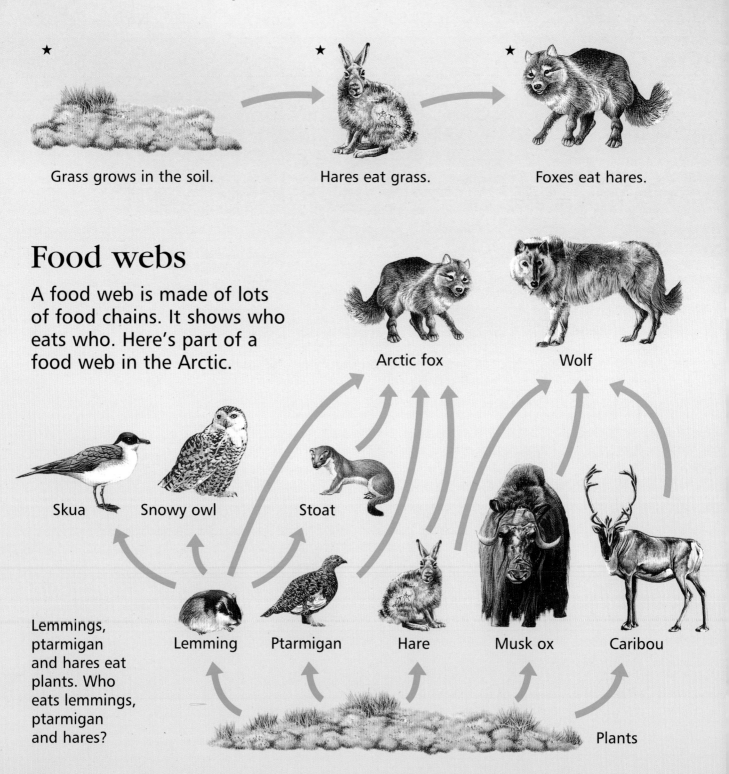

★

Grass grows in the soil.

★

Hares eat grass.

★

Foxes eat hares.

Food webs

A food web is made of lots of food chains. It shows who eats who. Here's part of a food web in the Arctic.

Arctic fox

Wolf

Skua

Snowy owl

Stoat

Lemmings, ptarmigan and hares eat plants. Who eats lemmings, ptarmigan and hares?

Lemming

Ptarmigan

Hare

Musk ox

Caribou

Plants

Sharing food

Different animals can live together in one place, even if they all eat plants. There's enough food to go around because they eat in different ways. This is how some grassland animals share plants.

Giraffes use their long necks to reach up to leaves and twigs from the tops of trees.

Male giraffes stretch up to eat.

Female giraffes eat leaves near to their mouths.

Elephants stretch up with their trunks to grab leaves and twigs, or down to pull up grass.

Gerenuks can stand on their back legs to eat the top leaves of bushes.

Warthogs feed on grass or dig up roots to eat.

Dik-diks eat the lowest part of bushes.

Rhinoceroses munch on leaves from bushes at the same level as their heads.

World in danger

There are many things we do to our world that put animals, plants and people in danger.

Smoke and fumes from factories and cars pollute the air.

Rainforest damage

Every year, huge areas of rainforests are cut down or burned. This is done for the wood, and to make space for farms. It destroys the homes of the animals that live there.

These rainforest trees are being burned to make space for farming.

Pollution

Litter, smoke from factories and cars, and oil spilled from ships at sea are all kinds of pollution. Pollution harms animals and people and the places where they live.

★ Litter looks horrible and can be dangerous for wildlife.

★ Chemicals from factories and farms can get into the water and soil.

★ Oilspills from ships can harm sea animals.

Animals in danger

Some animals are endangered – there are only a few of them left and they could easily die out. This is because we have hunted them or destroyed the places where they live.

Rhinos are killed for their horns. This one has had its horns cut off so hunters will leave it alone.

Golden lion tamarins became endangered when rainforests were cut down.

Some types of leopards are endangered because people hunt them for their skins.

Fishing dangers

When fishermen catch too many fish of the same kind, the number of fish starts to go down. This is called overfishing. If this doesn't stop soon, some kinds of fish will die out completely. Fishing can also endanger ocean life in other ways.

Purse seine nets are like big bags. They are used to catch tuna fish, but dolphins often get caught in the nets by mistake.

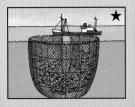

Trawl nets drag along the seabed to catch fish. They also pull up plants, and so destroy the homes of many sea creatures.

World map

This map shows the world's seas and oceans, its seven continents, climates and biggest cities. Do you know where you live on this map?

World climates

Climate is the usual kind of weather an area has. The different shaded areas on this map show these different climates:

◼ Mountains – cold for much of the year

◻ Polar climate – very cold all year

◼ Temperate climate – some rain in all seasons

◻ Warm climate – summers are hot and dry, winters are mild and wet

◻ Desert climate – hot and very dry all year

◼ Tropical climate – hot all year, with heavy rain in the wet season

◼ Equatorial climate – hot and wet with rain every day

NORTH AMERICA

Atlantic Ocean

SOUTH AMERICA

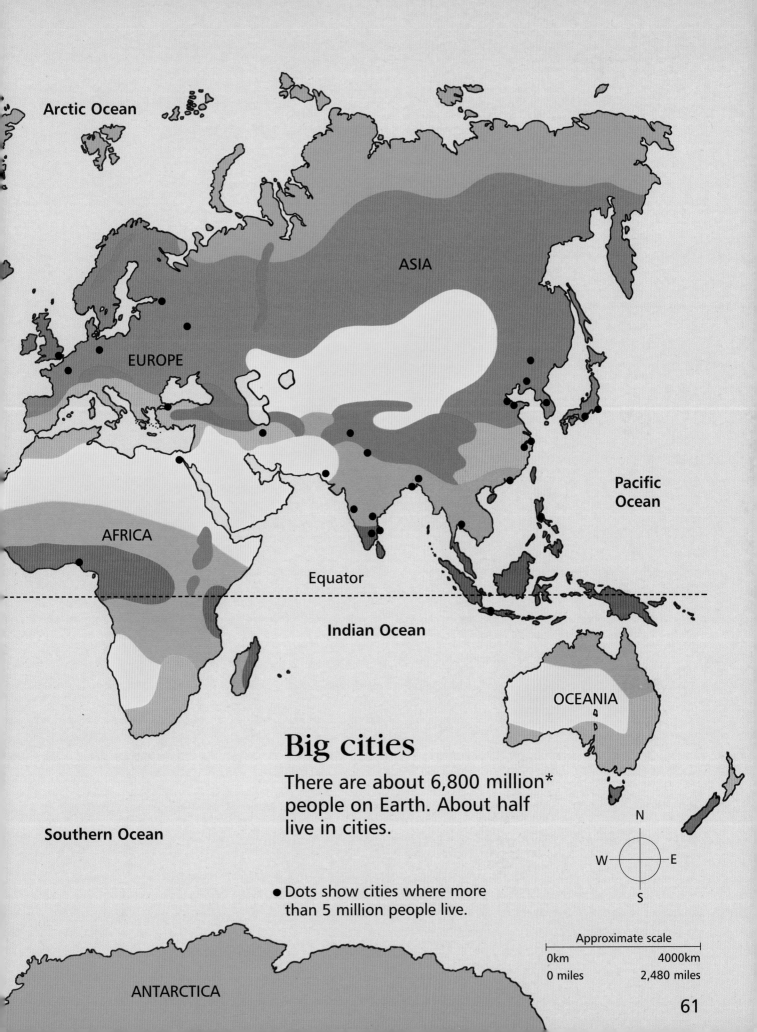

Arctic Ocean

ASIA

EUROPE

AFRICA

Pacific
Ocean

Equator

Indian Ocean

Big cities

There are about 6,800 million*
people on Earth. About half
live in cities.

Southern Ocean

OCEANIA

N
W — E
S

● Dots show cities where more
than 5 million people live.

Approximate scale

0km	4000km
0 miles	2,480 miles

ANTARCTICA

Index

Acknowledgements

The publishers are grateful to the following for permission to reproduce material:
front cover leaves, © Michael Luque/SPL; background and peguins, © Digital Vision; butterflies, © Dr. John Brackenbury/SPL;
illustrations by Adam Larkum; back cover polar bear, © Digital Vision; p4 globe, © Digital Vision; p5 Earth, © Digital Vision; p9
Saturn 5, © NASA; p10 Landsat, © Digital Vision; hurricane, © NASA Goddard Space Flight Center; city, © Digital Vision; sea
temperatures, © CLRC, Rutherford Appleton Laboratory; p11 shuttle, © CORBIS; p12 sunrise, © Digital Vision; sunset, © Digital
Vision; p13 Sun behind clouds, © Digital Vision; p16 sunflowers, © Getty Images/Tony Stone; wind, © Getty Images/Tony Stone;
snow, © Getty Images/Tony Stone; p17 clouds (from Met. Office), © R.D.Whyman; snowflakes, © NOAA/Dept of Commerce;
p18 tornado, © Getty Images/Tony Stone; lightning, © Digital Vision; hurricane damage, © Will and Deni McIntyre/SPL; p22
house after earthquake, © Joseph Sohm, ChromoSohm/CORBIS; p24 volcano, © Digital Vision; house on fire, © Digital Vision;
p.24–25 lava, © Digital Vision; p25 Surtsey volcano, © Geoscience Picture Library; p27 waterfall, © Kevin R. Morris/CORBIS; p29
Indian monsoon, © Getty Images/Tony Stone; rice paddy, © Getty Images/Tony Stone; p30–31 mountains, © Digital Vision; p31
avalanche, © Rex Features; p34 Pacific, © Tom Van Sant, Geosphere project/Planetary Visions/SPL; fishing boy, © Julian Cotton/
Powerstock; trawler and net, © Getty Images/Tony Stone; creels, © Scottish Highland Photo Library/J Macphearson; p40–41
caves, © Arne Hodalic/CORBIS; p45 wheat fields, © Ron Watts/CORBIS; p48–49 penguins and icebergs, © Digital Vision; p51
crevass, © CORBIS; p52–53 Central Park, © Patrick Batchelder/ Alamy; p53 traffic jam, © Jeremy Horner/CORBIS; p55
wind turbines, © Digital Vision; solar panels, © Chinch Gryniewicz, Ecoscene/CORBIS; dam, Digital Vision; p58 factories,
© Digital Vision; trees, © Digital Vision; p59 leopard, © Digital Vision.
Every effort has been made to trace and acknowledge ownership of copyright. If any rights have been omitted,
the publishers offer to rectify this in any subsequent editions following notification.

This edition updated by Lisa Jane Gillespie and Lisa Verrall • Cover design: Stephen Moncrieff • Digital artwork: Michèle Busby
and Nicola Butler • Picture researcher: Ruth King • Editorial development: Kamini Khanduri • Assistant editor: Rosie Heywood